IRRECONCILABLE!

A Study of the
Pharisees and Their Conflict With Jesus

By Gary P. Baumler

NORTHWESTERN PUBLISHING HOUSE
Milwaukee, Wisconsin

Design: Lynda Williams

Cover Image: from *Die Bibel in Bildern* (1860)
by Julius Schnorr von Carolsfeld

Northwestern Publishing House
N16W23379 Stone Ridge Dr., Waukesha, WI 53188-1108
www.nph.net

Published 2022
Printed in the United States of America
ISBN 978-0-8100-3171-5

22 23 24 25 26 27 28 29 30 31 10 9 8 7 6 5 4 3 2 1

Gary P. Baumler

IRRECONCILABLE!

A Study of the **Pharisees and Their Conflict With Jesus**

IRRECONCILABLE!

A Study of the

Pharisees and Their Conflict With Jesus

STUDENT LESSON

A downloadable leader's guide (2201202E) with PDF and RTF files and a promotional toolkit is available separately online at **nph.net**.

Lesson 1

> **"For I [Jesus] tell you that unless your righteousness surpasses that of the Pharisees and the teachers of the law, you will certainly not enter the kingdom of heaven."** (Matthew 5:20)

Setting the Stage

Drawing on your understanding of Scripture, discuss this question: Why would anyone in Jesus' day or today be irreconcilably opposed to Jesus? See 1 Corinthians 1:23; 2:13; and John 6:42; 11:47,48.

Origin

Their reputation had preceded them. When John saw many of the Pharisees and Sadducees coming to where he was baptizing, he knew they were not ready for what he had to offer. He lashed out at them, calling them "a brood of vipers" and asking why they thought they belonged there. He ordered them to "produce fruit in keeping with repentance" (Matthew 3:7-11).

Odd that John would say that of them! The Pharisees in particular lived outwardly upright lives. They were models of what a follower of God should look like. No one was more meticulous about following the ways of God than a good Pharisee. What "fruit" could they possibly lack?

The answer to that question is at once simple and horribly complicated—a story wrapped up in human paradox. Those who favor the Pharisees see them as the best of the best spiritual leaders. Others, reacting to accounts in the New Testament, condemn them as pious hypocrites. Scholars on both sides challenge the findings of the others. Nevertheless, the conflict that played out between not just John but Jesus and the Pharisees was by all accounts *irreconcilable.*

1. You will learn much more about the Pharisees, but from what you know already, what traits do you see in them that some would consider worth emulating? What traits would lead others to call them hypocrites?

The seeds of this conflict were planted many years before the encounter between John and the Pharisees and Sadducees at the Jordan River. We see them flowering during the years between the Old and the New Testaments when the Pharisees, the Sadducees, and the Essenes began to emerge as the political, spiritual, and ideological leaders among the Jews who had returned from the Babylonian captivity.

During captivity and the years following, the Jews had to deal with new challenges and threats. For much of that time they no longer had the temple of God—the place where God commanded them to carry out their sacrifices and where he confirmed his presence among them—for the center of their worship. They were wanting for spiritual direction.

2. Discuss the aspects of temple worship that were meant to help the people understand God's plan of salvation for them.

Gradually, synagogues sprung up where they could gather for prayer and teaching. The synagogues did not replace the temple, but they became centers that began to reshape the direction of their religion. The Pharisees, moreover, felt that by keeping the laws of God relating to the temple they, in effect, brought the temple directly into their everyday lives. They exercised considerable influence in the synagogues.

3. Discuss how the lack of a temple would shape the thinking of the Pharisees.

Once set free from Babylon (then under Persian rule) to return to Jerusalem, the Jews soon also encountered new enemies; in particular, the Romans. At the time of Jesus, the Israelites were a vassal state under Roman rule. They had some level of local control, but they had to yield ultimate control to the handpicked rulers of Rome and pay exorbitant taxes to Rome.

Of the three major philosophical sects among the Jews, the Essenes had the least direct impact upon the society. They lived in communes and practiced stringent, personal rules of life and conduct—much like we might associate with monasteries. The Scriptures do not speak of the Essenes directly.

The Pharisees and Sadducees, on the other hand, exercised considerable influence over the people. Depending on which group enjoyed the favor of the Roman puppet ruler, that group enjoyed political power. The religious influence, however, belonged primarily to the Pharisees. By the time of Jesus, the Sadducees held most of the local political power, but the Pharisees dominated in religious matters.

4. As you read through the following section, look for reasons the Pharisees would be favored among the common people over the Sadducees.

The high priests, who held the leadership in the Jewish ruling council (the Sanhedrin), were Sadducees. The Pharisees, however, enjoyed considerable influence with the common people and, as a result, with the Sadducees. To feel secure in their favored ruling positions, the Sadducees could not afford to lose the favor of the common people by openly opposing the Pharisees.

No one ever accused the Sadducees themselves of going out of their way to win the favor of the common people. Generally rude and boorish, they were patricians, wealthy aristocrats, and elitists who drew closer to the Roman occupiers than to their own people.

It is tempting to call the Sadducees conservative because they worked within the political status quo, happy to get along with the Romans occupying their land. However, cozying up to the Romans did not help their popularity, since most of the Jews hated the foreigners. Also, they claimed to accept the books of Moses (the Torah, or "teaching") literally, not adding anything to the text as the Pharisees did.

Their conservative stand on the Torah, however, was something of a sham. In truth, the Sadducees didn't seem to believe much of anything. They did not believe that God was in any way directly involved with people's everyday lives. They denied the resurrection of the dead or any afterlife and denied the existence of a spirit world with angels and demons (Matthew 22:23; Acts 23:8). A secular spirit pervaded the thinking of the Sadducees, and they sympathized with the pagan culture of the outsiders.

Meanwhile, the Pharisees also claimed allegiance to the Torah (the five books of Moses, Genesis to Deuteronomy). That allegiance, however, included what they called the "oral Torah." The laws in the five books of Moses, they said, were never meant to be static—the written word alone. Instead, Moses supposedly also passed on oral teachings and a practice of expanding the oral traditions over time. That way the Jews would keep the laws of the Torah relevant to the times. The new teachings did not replace the Torah, but they stood alongside it and, in fact, became the new moral norm. As long as they were permitted to teach and practice the Torah, the Pharisees were also tolerant of the Roman rule.

5. What is dangerous about the view of the oral Torah?

6. What examples of religious teaching do you see today that follow the pattern of the oral Torah?

According to the ancient historian Josephus (A.D.[1] 37–100), the Pharisees had "a reputation of excelling the rest of their nation in the observance of religion, and as exact exponents of the laws."[2] They claimed the authority to determine the meaning and requirements of the Torah.

7. The high moral standing and the religious authority of the Pharisees can hardly be overemphasized. Why would the teachings of the Pharisees logically appeal to the people?

Before and during Jesus' lifetime but prior to his public ministry, two schools of Jewish thought arose that largely shaped the Pharisees' thinking: the schools of Hillel (died A.D. 20) and Shammai (died A.D. 30). Shammai taught a strict adherence to the oral Torah and favored severe penalties for failure to obey. Some suggest that the particular Pharisees who opposed Jesus, and he them, were followers of the Shammai school of thought.

In contrast to Shammai, Hillel made a name as a lover of peace and for being gentle. He employed democratic principles that served to involve and elevate the laity. He grew in popularity, helping to solidify the Pharisees' popularity with the people. He spoke out against oppression and appeared as a defender of the people. He was by all accounts merciful, modest, and charitable. Some describe him as Jesus-like—or, since Jesus taught later, Jesus as Hillel-like. That being said, the differences between the schools of Shammai and Hillel were not dramatic. Hillel, by some accounts, could be every bit as strict as Shammai.

The followers of the Hillel and Shammai schools often debated their differences. The debates, however, did not cause a rift because, following each debate, the Jewish council decided which teaching to accept. Most of the time, Hillel's ideas prevailed. Each side accepted the judgment and lived to debate another day.

1 Some historians use the designations C.E., common era, and B.C.E., before the common era, instead of A.D. and B.C.

2 Quoted by Jacob Neusner, *From Politics to Piety: The Emergence of Pharisaic Judaism*, p. 51.

Points to Ponder

1. What fruit did the Pharisees lack?

2. What hint does Matthew 5:20 (at the head of this section) give you about the need for the Pharisees to produce "fruit in keeping with repentance" (Matthew 3:8)?

3. Again with reference to Matthew 5:20, why might the Pharisees' influence over the common people be a problem? Compare with Luke 9:48 and 10:21.

4. In sermons, you likely have heard us believers compared to Pharisees, warned of the danger of being like the Pharisees, or perhaps even pronounced guilty of the sin of the Pharisees. If the Pharisees are shown in such poor light in Scripture, why do we follow in their footsteps—why do we have to be warned?

Lesson 2

"For truly I [Jesus] tell you, until heaven and earth disappear, not the smallest letter, not the least stroke of a pen, will by any means disappear from the Law until everything is accomplished."
(Matthew 5:18)

Setting the Stage

Sometimes after visiting churches of other denominations, whether for a wedding, funeral, or as a guest of a relative, people have been heard to say, "That sounded just like a sermon that might have been preached at our church." How do you account for the similarities, even though the denominations may stand for very different teachings?

Jesus, a Pharisee?

1. As you read through this section, look for reasons some historians suggest that Jesus was a Pharisee. (Write your answers under Question 6.)

Likening Jesus to Hillel in the previous section is not a typo. Yes, some have wondered whether Jesus was a Pharisee. Consider, for example, that Hillel stated a version of the Golden Rule before Jesus did. It is said that Hillel was challenged to summarize the law while standing on one foot. He replied, "That which is hateful to you, do not do to your fellow. That is the whole Torah, the rest is only its explanation."[3] Jesus, in his Sermon on the Mount, said, "So in everything, do to others what you would have them do to you, for this sums up the Law and the Prophets" (Matthew 7:12).

This observation immediately raises the question of who or what influenced whom. In truth, the Golden Rule was around long before the Pharisees. One of the earliest references to it belongs to the pagan Confucius (551–479 B.C.) who said, "What you do not want done to yourself, do not do to others."[4]

When you think about it, the Golden Rule just makes common sense. The significant sameness between Hillel and Jesus, however, appears in the assertion that this teaching speaks to the very essence of law—Hillel: "the whole Torah"; Jesus: "sums up the Law and the Prophets."

So, this truth, spoken early by a pagan, is important enough to raise the question: Where did it originate?

The first answer that comes to mind: It came from God.

The follow-up question must be this: How did Confucius, not to mention anyone else, get it from God?

What is called common sense above suggests God's answer. Those who do not have God's law as we find it in the Bible have it "written on their hearts." The apostle Paul calls it "conscience" (Romans 2:15). Our consciences help make us conscious of this fundamental truth of God's law. What some know only from conscience, however, Jesus knew from his Father in heaven.

Nevertheless, we see from this sameness between Hillel and Jesus—both of whom reference Scripture—that the things Jesus

3 Quoted in several sources listed on the addenda page.

4 Quoted by C. Safrai in *Hillel and Jesus,* edited by Charlesworth and Johns, p. 373. (You may have noticed one difference between Jesus' words and those of Hillel and Confucius. They state the rule in the negative, Jesus in the positive. The negative comes out sounding self-centered, self-protective. What Jesus taught is clearly focused on what you should do for others—it is other-person focused.)

taught did not always conflict with what the Pharisees taught. Other occasions also seem to point to similarities and concord rather than opposition and conflict between the teachings of the Pharisees and Jesus.

2. Explain this statement: The fact that the unbeliever Confucius spoke words that were a form of the Golden Rule, hundreds of years before Jesus, doesn't invalidate what Jesus said.

The earliest public contact with Jesus and the Pharisees did not appear confrontational on the surface, although what was hidden below the surface would soon appear. The Pharisees came from all over Israel to hear Jesus' teaching (Luke 5:17). There is no hint that they were anything less than genuinely curious to hear him. Even when they questioned his authority to forgive the sins of a paralyzed man (5:21) and later his eating with "tax collectors and sinners" (5:30), nothing suggests any lack of sincerity in their questions. They may even have joined in praising God following the healing (5:26). That would change soon enough, however, since they did not accept his answers to their questions.

Meanwhile, on three occasions, Pharisees invited Jesus to their homes to eat with them (Luke 7:36; 11:37; 14:1). Their motives may not have seemed honorable in every case; the Pharisees were not likely to invite an avowed enemy into their homes. They normally did not associate with non-Pharisees.

Furthermore, on one occasion, some Pharisees also came to Jesus to warn him that Herod was plotting to kill him (Luke 13:31).

3. Given what you now know about the Pharisees, what might have been the motive behind these invitations to dine at their homes?

Some will also point to Jesus' discourse with the Pharisees as being very Pharisee-like, in the style of Shammai versus Hillel. The oral traditions were never considered static or unchangeable but were regularly debated. The traditions were used to interpret the Torah for the present day—to answer questions left unanswered by Moses in the Torah.

The traditions served yet another function. They built a "fence"[5] around the Torah, thus protecting it and its followers from abuse. They attempted to make it virtually impossible to seriously or unwittingly violate the Mosaic law. If the law commanded rest on the Sabbath, they felt the need to define—often in minutest detail—what was work that would violate the Sabbath.

4. Putting the best construction on everything, make a case for the oral traditions, explaining how the Pharisees might sincerely believe that they were helpful.

5 Rabbinic tradition written in the Talmud and quoted in several sources: "Be deliberate in judgment, and raise up many disciples; and make a fence for the Torah."

5. What is the flaw in the rationale that building a fence around the law is a good thing?

So, they debated details never mentioned by Moses, such as limiting a Sabbath Day's journey to two thousand cubits—a bit less than two-thirds of a mile, or forbidding sifting and kneading to make bread. In matters of cleanliness and purification, schools of Shammai and Hillel argued "whether the hands were to be washed before the cup was filled with wine, or after that, and where the towel was to be deposited."[6] As to tithing, they were not to use or partake of anything that had not been tithed.

Certainly, the Pharisees required some extreme measures when expanding and applying the Mosaic laws, particularly in reference to the Sabbath, tithing, and cleanliness. Still, some would say that they see parallels in some of Jesus' teachings. His sermon recorded in Matthew 5–7[7] serves as a prime example. There, Jesus emphasizes that he did not "come to abolish the Law," which some interpret to mean the oral law (The Pharisees conveniently ignore the concluding words of Jesus, "but to fulfill [it]") (5:17). He puts anger and calling someone a fool on a level with murder (5:21,22). He equates lustful looks with adultery and speaks of gouging out your eye if it causes you to "stumble" (5:27-30). Do not "swear an oath." "Turn . . . the other cheek." "Love your enemies." "Be perfect, therefore, as your heavenly Father is perfect" (5:33-48).

So, some make the case that Jesus was, or at least acted and taught like, a Pharisee.

6 Edersheim, *The Life and Times of Jesus the Messiah,* Vol. II, p. 210.

7 Often referred to as the Sermon on the Mount.

6. As you have read through this section, what reasons have you uncovered that have led some historians to wonder whether Jesus was a Pharisee?

The thought never surfaces that, by sounding like a Pharisee, Jesus was actually demonstrating the flaw in their thinking about the law. The Pharisees saw the law as a guide to living, but they did not see it as a mirror that reflected their hopeless sinfulness and need for a Savior. Yes, God's laws apply down to the minutest detail and in ways the Pharisees never thought of, but no, they could never perfectly fulfill them as they thought they could—not even with a dash of God's mercy thrown in. But that's a subject for a later chapter.

Finally, we certainly realize that not all Pharisees fell under the damning wrath of Jesus. Some Pharisees turned to Jesus and became Christians. Think of Nicodemus, who came to Jesus in secret by night. He learned from Jesus the sure comfort of the gospel (John 3). To Nicodemus, Jesus spoke the most often cited words of the New Testament Scriptures: "For God so loved the world that he gave his one and only Son, that whoever believes in him shall not perish but have eternal life" (John 3:16).

Nicodemus, it appears, heard and believed. At first, however, he remained a secret disciple of Jesus out of fear. The other Pharisees would see to it that he was cast out of the synagogue if they knew. That was a dreaded punishment for a Pharisee, equivalent to being cast out of God's kingdom. Yet Nicodemus went public as a Christian when he, along with Joseph of Arimathea (another Christian Pharisee), later claimed the body of Jesus from the cross for burial.

Other lesser-known Pharisees also became Christians and carried some Pharisaic baggage along with them. They still wanted to enforce the laws of circumcision for gentile Christians, although those laws no longer applied (Acts 15:5ff). And, of course, we have in the apostle Paul the most outstanding example of a Pharisee turned Christian. Paul had studied under the popular Pharisee Gamaliel, who later also interceded for the apostles when the Jewish council wanted to put them to death (Acts 5:17-42).

7. Though these Pharisees believed that Jesus was the promised Messiah, why do you think they stumbled over the issue of the enforcement of the Old Testament laws?

8. The apostle Paul had been a rising star among the Pharisees. Explain his observation in Philippians 3:4-8.

We will return to Paul later, since he deserves closer attention when it comes to discussing the Pharisees. Meanwhile, we have included this chapter in an attempt to reflect some of the history and thinking of scholars, including some present-day Jewish scholars who are more sympathetic to the Pharisees than most Christians are likely to be.

Points to Ponder

1. Compare and contrast the quote from Matthew 5:18, which introduces this chapter, with the Pharisees' intent to build a fence around the law.

2. Read Luke 7:36-50; 15:1,2. Take note that Jesus ate with known sinners on occasion and Pharisees on other occasions. What parallels or differences can you decipher from these accounts?

3. Page through the Sermon on the Mount (Matthew 5–7) and point out more places that Jesus emphasized the finer points of God's law. Pay attention to 5:17. What is especially important about that verse?

4. The Pharisees who believed in Jesus but insisted on strict adherence to the Old Testament law are called Judaizers. Today many Christians believe that the essence of the Christian message is that we become more Christlike. In what ways are the two groups similar?

Lesson 3

When the teachers of the law who were Pharisees saw him eating with the sinners and tax collectors, they asked his disciples: "Why does he eat with tax collectors and sinners?" (Mark 2:16)

Setting the Stage

In a number of places, the Bible warns us to avoid those who might hurt us spiritually. Read Psalm 1:1,2. Give examples of how you might apply these words to your life.

What thoughts or principles in these two verses would appeal to a Pharisee?

The Separatists

A strong hint to understanding the Pharisees and their clash with Jesus lies in their name. It comes from the Hebrew word *Perusim,* which means "separated ones." They separated themselves from the Gentiles, from non-Pharisaic Jews, and in particular from the common people, known by the term "people of the earth" (Hebrew "am ha-aretz"). Thinking of the Pharisees' strong emphasis on rules of cleanliness, one could say that they literally considered those people as the great unwashed common folk among the Jews.

The Pharisees, nevertheless, and in spite of their apparent disdain for them, exercised—as noted earlier—considerable influence over the common people. In the synagogues, the Pharisees taught a strong religious ethic. With little or no emphasis on doctrinal questions, they addressed the question: How should we live? They expounded the so-called oral Torah.

1. The emphasis on "How should we live?" is a key concept in understanding the Pharisees. That sounds like a wholesome question for a God-fearing person to ask. From what you already know about the Pharisees, what went wrong or where did they veer from the truth?

2. At one time, "What Would Jesus Do?" was a favorite slogan or question some Christians asked to help them decide what they should do or how they should react to whatever situation they faced. That too sounds like a logical and wholesome question to ask. What danger, however, is there in focusing on that refrain?

The Pharisees' separation from and influence over the common people made them inherently hypocritical. It is true that they spoke out against hypocrisy, condemning it also within their own ranks.

They also called for humility. Still, in practice, their separation from everyone *unclean* fostered a better-than-thou spirit, which is hypocritical on its face.

Jesus exposed that spirit in his parable of the Pharisee and the tax collector (Luke 18:9-14). The Pharisee in the parable could readily count the ways he was separated from other people—including the vile tax collector standing in abject humility at a distance. The Pharisee was quick to remind God of how he fasted and tithed. The Pharisee had concluded, as did the people to whom Jesus told the parable (v. 9), that what he did in obeying the law made him right with God. He could see no flaws in himself, certainly not the flaw of his contempt for others who did not live up to the same standards as he.

Meanwhile, the tax collector in true humility cast his eyes downward, pounded his chest, and cried, "God, have mercy on me a sinner."[8] He did not try to offer any evidence that he should be considered right with God. He did not offer God a life worth saving but called for mercy from him who alone could save. Then Jesus spoke the verdict: "I tell you that this man, rather than the other, went home justified before God" (v. 14).

3. Both the Pharisee and tax collector understood that a holy God commanded and deserved righteous obedience to his law. Summarize the essential difference in the way the two men believed they would achieve righteousness.

The Pharisees, in separating from the Gentiles, reflected yet another flaw in their thinking that drove a wedge between them and Jesus. In their separation, they misunderstood and misapplied what it meant for them to be the children of Abraham. Instead of recognizing that their birthright from God was the promise of the Messiah to be born of Jewish parents, specifically parents in the line of King David, they saw it as a bloodline that preserved a favorable relationship with God.

8 There is a significant small word missing in this translation, the word *the*. The tax collector called himself, personally, "the sinner." He made no comparisons with others.

4. Read Genesis 12:1-3. Identify and explain the words that point to the significance of what it meant to be children of Abraham.

John the Baptist pinpointed that flaw in the Pharisees and Sadducees already when they came to where he was preaching and baptizing. After he denounced them as a brood of vipers, he warned: "Do not think you can say to yourselves, 'We have Abraham as our father' " (Matthew 3:9).

Jesus also laid bare the problem of the Jews—considering their legacy as children of Abraham as a spiritual badge of honor. When he called for them to learn and hold to his teachings—"and the truth will set you free"—they countered, "We are Abraham's descendants and have never been slaves of anyone" (John 8:31-33).

Jesus drove his point home: "I tell you, everyone who sins is a slave to sin" (John 8:34). He said, furthermore, that by choosing Abraham over him they actually separated themselves from Abraham and him.

"Abraham is our father," they insisted (John 8:39). By clinging to Abraham in this way, they followed another father but not Abraham—no, and not God.

5. Read John 8:34-39. What was Jesus referring to when he said, "If you were Abraham's children, . . . then you would do what Abraham did"?

Yes, the Pharisees were, as their name indicated, separatists. But when they used their relationship with Abraham as a reason to reject Jesus as the Messiah sent from God the Father, they followed another father and separated themselves from God's truth. "You belong to your father, the devil," Jesus concluded (John 8:44).

Although the Pharisees are not specifically named in this part of the John 8 account, they were identified earlier (v. 13) and clearly were the ones who perpetuated that way of thinking. Besides, Jesus also said to these men, "I know that you are Abraham's descendants. Yet you are looking for a way to kill me, because you have no room for my word" (v. 37).

And who were the ones who wanted to kill Jesus? Following another encounter with Jesus, "the Pharisees went out and plotted how they might kill Jesus" (Matthew 12:14).

So, thinking it was enough to claim Abraham as their father, the separatists found themselves separated from the truth of God in Christ (the Messiah). The clash between the Pharisees and Jesus could hardly have been more severe. They claimed he was in league with the devil. He told them they were sons of the devil. He said that they did not know God or else they would know and believe him. They tried to kill him (John 8:48-59).

Points to Ponder

1. Read Matthew 7:15 and Romans 16:17 (compare also Romans 12:16 and the quote at the beginning of this lesson, Mark 2:16). Compare and contrast the separation called for by God and the activity of the Pharisees that earned them their name as separatists.

2. Read the full text of John 8:31-47 and comment further on how the Pharisees misapplied their physical descent from Abraham (compare with Romans 4:16).

3. Conservative Lutherans are often known for being against this or that. Of course, there are scriptural reasons for being against anything that might promote false teaching or against someone who promotes sin. However, if we focus most on what we are against, it is easy to slide into hypocrisy and self-righteousness. Describe the narrow Lutheran middle way that will help us keep from accepting false teaching or sin or from becoming self-righteous.

Lesson 4

> **"[The Jewish people] have known me [Paul] for a long time and can testify . . . that I conformed to the strictest sect of our religion, living as a Pharisee."**
> (Acts 26:5)

Setting the Stage

Think of two examples of how Christians in general, and perhaps you specifically, have been accused of ignorance or lack of love for speaking out against something.

The apostle Paul stood in strong opposition to the Pharisees' position on the law. Some view his opposition as a result of ignorance.

Paul the Pharisee

Following Jesus' death and resurrection, a Pharisee came on the scene who carried an antagonism against all things having to do with Christ. This man's most fervent ambition was to capture and kill Christians. He was Saul, whom we first see at the stoning of Stephen: "Saul approved of their killing him" (Acts 8:1).

1. What was it about the early Christians that stirred up such animosity among the Pharisees that they could condone killing the Christians?

Saul, as we know, was later miraculously converted to believe in and serve Christ. We know him better as Paul, the Greek form of his name that he apparently preferred after his conversion to Christianity. We know him also as an apostle of Christ, a world missionary for Christ, and the inspired writer of numerous New Testament letters.

Through Paul we can see even more clearly why the Pharisees opposed the message being taught by the Christians.

2. Read Acts 13:38,39,46,47. What two issues did the Pharisees consider to be especially repulsive?

3. What strong claims did Paul make about those who followed the teachings of the Pharisees? Read Galatians 3:10,11.

Some Jewish apologists, however, counter Paul's claims against the Pharisees by asserting that he never understood the Pharisees and was, therefore, the wrong person to comment on them. So we need to look more closely at Paul the Pharisee.

When Paul returned to Jerusalem following his final recorded missionary journey, some Jews from Asia stirred up the people against him. An uproar ensued, and they tried to kill him. The Roman soldiers intervened and arrested Paul. However, when they learned that he was a Roman citizen by birth, they quickly turned him over to the local Jewish council to settle the matter.

Once Paul had the chance to address the council, he called out to them, "My brothers, I am a Pharisee, descended from Pharisees" (Acts 23:6). What followed set off a violent dispute among the Jewish leaders about what to do about Paul. Once again, the Romans had to intercede.

4. Did Paul's avowal, "I am a Pharisee," somehow negate his stand against the Pharisees' position on the law? Explain.

You may want to look further in Acts 23 and beyond to see the eventual outcome of this event, but our attention is drawn to the claim he made for himself before the council: "I am a Pharisee." A few days later when brought before the Roman ruler, King Agrippa, Paul doubled down about being a Pharisee: "I conformed to the strictest sect of our religion, living as a Pharisee" (Acts 26:5).[9]

It is Paul's statement before the council that draws the attention, however. Writers point out that he said, "I am a Pharisee," not "I was a Pharisee" or "I used to be a Pharisee." Simply "I am." The argument follows: Here is a renowned Christian leader who is, at the same time, a Pharisee. See! Pharisaism and Christianity are compatible. In fact, some say Pharisaism set the foundation for Christianity.

9 Although Paul was trained by Gamaliel (Acts 5:34ff) in what may be considered a more moderate school of Pharisaism, he clearly chose the strictest path forward. In general, the differences between the schools of the Pharisees were considered as relatively minor.

5. Read Acts 26:4-6,9,10,14-18. From this context discuss whether Paul still considered himself to be a Pharisee in the sense that some have claimed he did.

When you know Paul and his teachings, you plainly see that the law-focused message of the Pharisees was not compatible with the gospel Paul taught. To understand Paul's claim here, look closer at the context. Paul had been thrust into an unfair hearing of the Jewish council based on accusations that he was teaching everywhere against the Jews. He stood before the Pharisees and Sadducees who, as we saw earlier, opposed each other on key teachings of Scripture—the most important being the resurrection of the dead. So he took his stand by siding with the Pharisees—"I am a Pharisee"—and pointed out that he agreed with the truth of the resurrection of the dead. His words set off the dispute between the Sadducees and Pharisees in the council.

6. Some regard Paul's claim, "I am a Pharisee," to be a confession of faith. Others wonder if it was more of a diversionary tactic to draw attention away from himself. Explain the rationale behind each supposition.

Paul had not said that he agreed at that time with all of the teachings and ways of the Pharisees, and speaking of his Pharisaism to King Agrippa later, he described it in the past. Writing at a later date to the Philippians, he repeated his claim that he once had a zeal for the law as strong as any Pharisee (Philippians 3:6).

7. Read Philippians 3:2-9. What significant change separated Paul from the strict Pharisee he had been?

8. Where did he find what changed him? What did he do to warrant what he gained, namely, righteousness?

Now, as a Christian, he drew some vitally important lessons from the law that the Pharisees missed. He had been "in regard to the law, a Pharisee" (Philippians 3:5). Yes, he described himself as every bit as self-righteous (confident in his flesh) as any Jew could claim.

Those who write in favor of the Pharisees fail, however, to mention the rest of Paul's thought that follows. What he thought he gained in his pharisaical life, working out his own righteousness based on the law, he now considered to be just so much "garbage" ("dung" in the King James Version, literally, "excrement"). He had found true righteousness—not of his own that comes by the law. Through faith in Christ, he had found "the righteousness that comes from God on the basis of faith" (Philippians 3:9).

Paul knew full well how the Pharisees used the law to justify themselves. He no longer was that kind of Pharisee. His plea before the Jewish council when he said, "I am a Pharisee," did not imply otherwise. His avowal was centered on his belief in the resurrection.

So then, what about the conclusion that Paul did not understand the Pharisees even though he claimed that he had been a super strict one? Their case, it seems, is based on how Paul felt about the way they used the law in their teachings and lives. They would deny Paul's characterization of the Pharisees' views. At the same time, the same critics of Paul clearly claim that the Pharisees taught that they could adequately fulfill the law themselves and they didn't need a Savior to do it for them. That is exactly what Paul said of the Pharisees.

Points to Ponder

1. Read Galatians 3:1-9. Paul had preached to the Galatians and converted many to Christianity, and then Jews had convinced them that they still had to abide by Old Testament laws. What was the point of Paul's statement that those who have faith are children of Abraham?

2. Paul characterized all the things he had focused on as garbage. Identify some of the garbage in your life that you may have pursued as having utmost value, but now as a child of Christ you understand it does not have value in your relationship with God.

3. Why was knowing Christ Jesus of greater value for Paul than anything else? Why is it of greatest value for you?

Lesson 5

> **"For out of the heart come evil thoughts—murder, adultery, sexual immorality, theft, false testimony, slander. These are what defile a person; but eating with unwashed hands does not defile them."**
> (Matthew 15:19,20)

Setting the Stage

Much Christian literature contains misleading statements that give the impression that we are capable of deciding to follow Jesus. Of course, we would like to think that our conversion resulted because the seed of goodness was alive within us and we were wise enough to choose Christ. But that isn't true, and when you think abouwt it, it isn't comforting either.

"Accept Christ today." What is wrong with that statement?

False teaching inevitably robs us of comfort. Why would this false teaching undermine our gospel comfort?

Read John 8:31-39. Which words underscore the truth that we are not able to make a decision for Christ?

Free Will

When Jesus condemned the Pharisees as slaves to sin, they totally missed his point because they thought they had the freedom in themselves to choose right or wrong. Similarly, Paul's statement that he could not depend on his own righteousness but needed the righteousness that comes from God in Christ did not make sense to Pharisees (and many people today).

Although the Pharisees recognized that they fell short of keeping all the laws perfectly, they did not believe they were inherently sinful.

The Pharisees' idea of free will conjures up an image of an old cartoon illustration. In it, the subject is caught in the dilemma of having to decide between doing what is right or what is wrong. A good angel sits on his right shoulder, trying to convince him to do right. An evil angel (the devil) sits on his left shoulder, tempting him to do wrong.

- As a description of the way we are by nature, that picture is flawed. Describe a more accurate picture.

The Pharisees likely would have more readily agreed with the cartoon. They taught that people have two forces within them, the one to choose good and the other to choose evil. As I. Abrahams, a distinguished Jewish scholar, stated it: "Pharisaism . . . placed the seat of good and evil, virtue and vice, equally in the heart."[10]

10 I. Abrahams, *Studies in Pharisaism and the Gospels,* p. 121.

The goal to gain and keep favor with God was to choose good. As they did so, they were working with God to secure their ultimate reward, their place as children of God.

R. Travers Herford, an apologist (defender) for Pharisaism, explained the Pharisees' position as follows: "Human beings have in them two impulses, inclinations, or tendencies called Yetzers: the good inclination (Yetzer hatob) and the evil inclination (Yetzer hara). A person, created with both, is not the helpless slave of either. He has the free will to choose either. This teaching is considered a major pillar of Pharisaism."[11]

Missing in their assumptions was the reality taught by Jesus in the Matthew passage above that by nature only evil resides in our hearts. Or, as Paul said it, "I know that good itself does not dwell in me, that is, in my sinful nature" (or "flesh") (Romans 7:18). We will, necessarily, return to this matter again later.

Points to Ponder

1. How might the following passages help a modern-day Pharisee understand that we don't have the freedom in ourselves to choose right or wrong?

- Ephesians 2:1

- Romans 3:10-12

- Ephesians 2:8,9

11 Herford, *The Pharisees,* pp. 155,156.

2. How did the Pharisees' idea of free will mislead them away from Jesus?

3. What basic scriptural truth nullifies their position?

4. How did the Pharisees' belief in free will lead to a doctrine of salvation by keeping the law?

5. In Matthew 12:34, Jesus called the Pharisees a brood of vipers. In Matthew 16:12, Jesus warned his disciples to guard against the yeast of the Pharisees. Why did Jesus speak so harshly against the Pharisees?

6. The Bible's description of the spiritual condition of the believer is different than that of the cartoon with the two angels sitting on our shoulders, but the Bible does describe a struggle between the old Adam and the new man in each of us. At first glance, those two pictures might seem to illustrate a similar truth. From your Bible knowledge, what is different?

7. If the Pharisees' idea of free will were correct, what two extremes might overwhelm our thoughts when we approach death and think of judgment day?

Lesson 6

> **"Nothing outside a person can defile them by going into them. Rather, it is what comes out of a person that defiles them."** (Mark 7:15)

Setting the Stage

Discuss how the following statement might be misunderstood or misapplied. "Repentance is necessary for salvation."

Repentance was a key issue for the Pharisees.

The Law and Repentance

The Pharisaic way, as suggested earlier, was all about how to live. They found the answers in the laws of Moses and the traditions they formed in the oral law. They did not feel as if their use of the law was self-serving in any reprehensible way. As noted earlier, they taught humility and spoke out against those lacking it. They based their observance of the law on their love for God. They called for anyone breaking the law to repent. That does not sound like what we heard from Paul earlier when he condemned the righteousness of the Pharisees based on the law. Why, if the Pharisees felt content in their self-righteousness, would they call for repentance?

Paul's condemnation of their righteousness seems at odds with their focus on humility and repentance but not because he did not understand the Pharisees. Rather, they did not understand what Paul had learned in Christ. To the Pharisees, religion was singularly focused on doing what was right under God. On that score, scholars draw a parallel with and claim influence by the Pharisees on most other religions, including Christianity. Before looking closer at what the Pharisees were missing, take a look at how apologists for the Pharisees explain their religion.

We return to the Pharisees' view of the Scriptures: namely, the Old Testament, particularly the books of Moses. They did not believe that God's revelation was confined to the written text. They sought to interpret the text and apply it to their times. In the process, the sages of their day—provided with "fresh inspiration from God"[12]—developed new traditions or, as we identified earlier, the oral Torah.

Although they believed the traditions were binding, they were also debatable and changeable. The Pharisees, however, did not intend to contradict or abolish the teachings of Moses but to fulfill them.

The plan of God, as the Pharisees saw it, was to make the world perfect. They explored what they needed to do to fulfill God's plan, believing that they could in fact do what God wanted. A famous saying of their day was "The Holy One, blessed be He, was pleased to make Israel able to acquire merit; wherefore He gave them much Torah and many mitzvoth" (commands).[13]

Any devout Pharisee clearly wanted to serve God with his life. Any lesser purpose for his deeds was unacceptable. He also believed that God would reward such service with his blessings. Those blessings might be realized with material prosperity and/or ultimate spiritual bliss.

Although a Pharisee might proudly declare how exemplary a life he was leading, he also knew that he needed to acknowledge his

12 Cited by R. Travers Herford, *The Pharisees,* p. 66.

13 Herford, p. 137. Cited also by others.

sins and repent of them. R. Travers Herford writes most forcefully of how serious the matter of repentance was for the Pharisees: "Repentance must be a real turning of the soul to God, not a mere verbal formal profession; and, where possible, it must be accompanied by acts of reparation and amends."[14]

1. Read Mark 7:15 (at the beginning of this lesson) and Matthew 15:7-9,20. Jesus' critique of the Pharisees helps identify what led the Pharisees to their idea of repentance. What were the underpinnings of their teachings about repentance? Explain the imagery in Mark 7:15.

Some of the tenets of Pharisaism do sound much like what a Christian might also say. Some will say that Pharisaism helped give birth to Christianity and continues to be a major influence among Christians.

Most people will not likely dispute pharisaical influences in Christian churches, which we will try to demonstrate later, but that influence is not a positive thing. Nor do the perceived commonalities between Pharisaism and Christianity speak to the essence of Christianity or to the irreconcilable conflict we alluded to at the outset of this study. A closer look now will demonstrate how sin and repentance are not, in fact, the same thing for a Pharisee as for a Christian.

What exactly did it mean for a Pharisee to repent? It meant, of course, that he knew he had not perfectly kept all of the laws he attributed to God. So, he had to turn to God in repentance in order to gain new faith and strength to do better. He believed in advance that God would—in effect—overlook his sin, recognize the act of repentance, and forgive him, thus enabling him to improve his life and gain his reward. Repentance, thus presented, is an act of a person to gain or earn something from God.

14 Herford, p. 166.

2. Does God overlook any of our sins in the way the Pharisees thought? If not, how are we saved? See Romans 8:7,8; 6:23; 3:23,24; and Isaiah 53:5.

What it means that repentance is an act of a person will become clearer when we see what was missing in the Pharisees' view of repentance. To begin, the Pharisees felt no need for salvation as taught in the New Testament, particularly in Paul's epistles. They also naturally missed the same teaching in the Old Testament. It follows that they never dealt with the absolute damnableness of sin and the impossibility of human beings to atone for their own sin. They did not come to grips with the inherent corruption of sin in humans from birth. As a result, by repenting of their sins, they looked to God for a push, as it were—call it *mercy*—to get them back on the path of working out their own salvation.

3. Refer back to John 8:31-47. Elaborate on why the Pharisees felt no need for a Savior.

Seeing no need for a Savior from sin, the Pharisees saw Jesus as only another human being, not as the Son of God. They felt content that they were dealing directly with God already and did not need Jesus. Nor did Jesus fit their concept of the Messiah.

It is not clear how actively the Pharisees looked for the promised Messiah. But what seems amply clear is that the only Messiah they could have accepted would have been one who would set up an earthly kingdom and lead the charge to make the world the perfect place they envisioned.

Earlier we saw how the Pharisees thought they could fulfill the law. We saw also that Jesus countered them by declaring, "I have not come to abolish [the Law] but to fulfill [it]" (Matthew 5:17). The Pharisees, however, not only failed to keep the law in the way God commanded, but they made things worse by adding their traditions to the law. Jesus did fulfill the law as he said—on our behalf and in our place. Because the Pharisees would not see how woefully they fell short, they could not see why they would need the Messiah to keep the law for them. According to a well-known image used by Jesus, they didn't think they were sick and therefore concluded that they did not need a doctor (Matthew 9:12,13).

Points to Ponder

1. What do the Scriptures teach about repentance? Read Mark 1:15; Luke 24:47; and Acts 20:21.

2. The definition of repentance that we learn in catechism begins with this statement: It is a change of mind about sin.

   Below is a list of sins. Describe the change of mind that takes place regarding these sins from the view of the sinful nature to that of the repentant sinner.

   Gossip:

   Lust:

Hatred:

Unkind words:

Coveting:

3. The Pharisees failed to recognize that Jesus was the Messiah. Describe how their failure had its roots in their mistaken understanding of repentance and sin.

4. If we aren't saved by keeping the law, why is the proclamation of law still important for us?

Lesson 7

Great peace have those who love your law, and nothing can make them stumble. I wait for your salvation, LORD, and I follow your commands.
(Psalm 119:165,166)

Setting the Stage

Talking about our faith with someone of another religion, especially a non-Christian religion, can be confusing if we don't have a mutual understanding of terms we are using.

For example, what are some different ways that people understand the term *grace*?

A different understanding of terms may have contributed to the Pharisees' mistaken beliefs.

The Pharisaic Psalm

The Pharisees did not see any need to be saved by anyone else but themselves as long as they followed God's will. They flatly rejected Jesus as the Messiah, the Savior, and the Son of God. Jesus did miracles, and the Pharisees said he was in league with the devil and faulted him when he healed on the Sabbath. Jesus raised the dead, and the Pharisees plotted to kill him. On trial for his life, Jesus avowed that he was "the Messiah, the Son of God." His accusers declared him guilty of blasphemy and ridiculed him (Matthew 26:63-67). Jesus rose from the dead, and the Jewish leaders devised a false narrative to deny it (Matthew 28:11-15).

The clash between the Pharisees and Jesus was inevitable, but some critics seem to imply that it was rather a clash between the Old Testament and the New Testament. As an example, writers point in particular to Psalm 119, which they say embodies everything that the Pharisees stood for, labeling it a "purely Pharisaic" psalm.[15]

Can we, therefore, accept the Old Testament as true in its entirety and still find fault with the Pharisees? Or is the New Testament a whole new revelation not connected to the Old Testament, and the Pharisees were merely carrying on with the Old Testament teachings and preserving them against the new?

It is easy to see why some claim that Psalm 119 is the psalm of the Pharisees. The opening words seem to support the claims of those who are favorably disposed toward the Pharisees. "Blessed are those whose ways are blameless, who walk according to the law of the LORD. Blessed are those who keep his statutes and seek him with all their heart" (Psalm 119:1,2).

1. Why would these statements be so appealing to the Pharisees?

2. Look at just the first two sections of the psalm (through verse 16). Pick out other words and phrases that Pharisees might hear as support for their position.

15 Term used by Herford about the psalm (p. 111), and a point referenced by several authors.

Let's look closer at the psalm to see if it, in fact, mirrors the life and teachings of the Pharisees. Without trying to do a study of all 176 verses of Psalm 119 (the longest chapter in the Bible), we can identify at least three issues related to that characterization.

First, consider how the use of the word *law* in the psalm contrasts with the Pharisees' use of it. It is the word *Torah,* which we have indicated means more literally "teaching." The psalmist also uses several other words in the psalm interchangeably with *Torah,* words in Hebrew that mean "testimonies," "precepts," "statutes," "commandments," "judgments," and "word." The problem is that the Pharisees seemed to see only the meaning of "law" in those terms.

These teachings, however, came from God in the books of Moses and any other Old Testament books that may have preceded this psalm. They encompass more than just laws but also the gospel. However, they do not include the self-proclaimed oral Torah of the Pharisees.

That leads to the second issue. Several thoughts in the psalm reveal gospel truths not present in the Pharisees' approach to the Torah. The psalmist, for example, implores God to give him "life" (Psalm 119:25). The law, however, has no power to give life.

3. Why doesn't the law have the power to give life?

Romans 3:20

Romans 4:15

Romans 1:16

Galatians 3:10

4. What hints do you see in verses 27 and 28 that when the psalmist speaks of God's precepts and his word, he is referring to more than law commands?

Among other words in the psalm that breathe the truth of the gospel—words like *peace* and *salvation*—perhaps the most telling occur in verses 174 and 176: "I long for your salvation, LORD. . . . I have strayed like a lost sheep." Those words do not reflect the spirit of the Pharisees. People who long for salvation and yet confess that they have strayed woefully (like perishing sheep) depend on God, not the merit of their works, for salvation.

The third and perhaps most significant issue: Other psalms, not to mention the books of Moses and the prophets, reveal our inherent unworthiness before God and also some of the promises fulfilled in Jesus the Messiah for our salvation.

Psalm 51 reads: "I know my transgressions, and my sin is always before me" (v. 3). "Surely I was sinful at birth, sinful from the time my mother conceived me" (v. 5). "Create in me a pure heart, O God" (v. 10). "Restore to me the joy of your salvation" (v. 12). "My sacrifice, O God, is a broken spirit" (v. 17).

5. Those who defend the Pharisees refer to Psalm 119 as the psalm of the Pharisees. Why could you legitimately label Psalm 51 as the psalm that condemns the Pharisees in their self-righteousness?

6. How could you use Psalm 22 to demonstrate that the Old and New Testaments are not two separate religious systems, but the continuous account of God's plan of salvation? (Compare with Matthew 27:46 and John 19:24.)

Certainly, we could delve more deeply into the many prophecies of the Messiah that were fulfilled in Jesus, but that is another study. What should be clear is that the Old Testament and New Testament not only were not in conflict, but the one complements and fulfills the other. Because they missed the connection, the unbelieving Pharisees created the conflict with Jesus.

Points to Ponder

1. Why wouldn't the Pharisees acknowledge or even recognize that Psalm 22 prophesied about the Messiah?

2. Many people believe that being a Christian is about being a better person—being more Christlike. Point out how Psalm 51 refutes that mistaken belief.

Lesson 8

"Woe to you experts in the law, because you have taken away the key to knowledge." (Luke 11:52)

Setting the Stage

Who hasn't heard warnings against silent killers—diseases or conditions that can be wreaking havoc in our bodies without our knowledge? High blood pressure, coronary artery disease, and diabetes are just a few examples of silent killers.

Jesus warned the disciples that the teaching of the Pharisees was the equivalent of a spiritual silent killer.

The Yeast (Leaven) of the Pharisees

The Pharisees and Sadducees dogged Jesus' heels, trying to trip him up. They feared the influence he had with the common people. They asked loaded questions about marriage, paying taxes, and Sabbath observances, but Jesus always gave an answer that befuddled them. As time passed, they became all the more determined to get rid of him.

Following one of those inquisitions (they asked him "to show them a sign from heaven"[16]), Jesus warned his disciples: "Be on your guard against the yeast of the Pharisees and Sadducees" (Matthew 16:5).

After some confusion about what Jesus meant about yeast, the disciples understood that Jesus was warning them to be on

16 Matthew 16:1. Jesus answered that they would get only "the sign of Jonah" (v. 4), a reference to Jesus' resurrection.

their guard against the teaching of the Pharisees and Sadducees (Matthew 16:5-12).

A basic meaning of the word *yeast* or *leaven* is "an element that permeates or transforms something," such as what happens when yeast makes bread dough rise. Jesus was warning that the teachings of the Pharisees and Sadducees would permeate the believers' thinking and transform their faith into something undesirable. Leaven starts small but spreads thoroughly. It functions unseen until it has done its work. Spiritually, it can destroy saving faith.

1. Read again the quote from Luke 11:52 that begins this lesson. The experts in the law were primarily Pharisees (Luke 11:37-54). Jesus said they have taken away the key to knowledge. Without yet addressing what the key to knowledge is, discuss how this condemnation illustrates the yeast image above.

Let's look first at the teaching of the Sadducees. From what we have discussed, we can conclude the following about their teaching: They denied the resurrection of the dead, the existence of the spirit world, and the interaction by God with the people on earth. Nevertheless, they claimed they accepted the unchanged text of the Torah as God's Word.

Such a contradictory position is yeast to be avoided. To embrace the Sadducees' teaching would mean to develop, at best, a careless approach to God's Word. Gradually nothing would be left for a person's faith to hold on to for salvation.

The leaven of this teaching starts working when people first begin to call into question any of the truths of Scripture, although they call it God's Word. This leaven often starts fermenting in connection with the miracles, at first questioning the seemingly insignificant accounts such as Jonah in the belly of a huge fish for three days.

Once leaven begins working, however, it doesn't stop as if satisfied with permeating just a corner of the dough. Similar challenges follow: Did God really part the Red Sea? Did Lot's wife really turn into a pillar of salt? Did God really create the world by the word of his mouth in just six normal days? Was Jesus really born of a virgin? Did Jesus really raise dead people? Did Jesus really rise from the dead? Was Jesus really the Messiah and the Son of God?

2. Read Proverbs 1:7; 3:13-18. What is the beginning of wisdom (1:7)? What does wisdom ultimately give those who embrace her (3:18)?

As such spiritual leaven works, clear and central teachings from God gradually fall by the way. At what point does a person have nothing left to believe for salvation, except perhaps some kind of a moral ethic?

This leads us quite naturally to look again at the teachings of the Pharisees. They taught a compelling religious ethic. They also held to some basic biblical teachings, such as belief in angels and the resurrection of the dead and a love for God and his law. How their teaching works as a leaven is not as obvious as the teaching of the Sadducees. For that reason, it is perhaps even more insidious.

The Pharisees did not appear to be contradicting or attacking biblical teachings as the Sadducees did, and yet they were tapping into the first sin, the desire to be like God. When Adam and Eve gave in to the devil's lies, they and their offspring were forever turned in on themselves. The fallback position for humans is "self" or "ego." "I'm okay!" "I've got this." "I don't need any help." "I am basically good."

3. What does it mean that the natural human fallback position is "self"?

In human affairs, that position often appears to work. We see people pulling themselves up by their own bootstraps. We applaud people who rise up from the ashes of failure, defeat, or bad beginnings and make something of themselves. We buy into the philosophy that everyone can be a winner. Who is to deny the evidence of many a success story?

There is, of course, an answer to that question. The signs of failure, desperation, and despair are all around us. Keep in mind that for every winner there is also a loser, usually many losers. Not all who strive succeed, but this line of talk could easily get us offtrack. The issue here is not about human success in this world; it is much more than that. It is about the basic human condition since sin corrupted our nature. It is about our need for temporal comfort and eternal welfare from outside of ourselves.

4. Where does the Pharisees' leaven or teaching lead us? Be prepared to illustrate.

Think again of what the Pharisees were missing. They paid close attention to God's command through Moses: "Be holy, because I am holy" (Leviticus 11:44,45). However, they seem to have missed the significance of God's declaration: "I am the LORD, who makes you holy" (Leviticus 20:8; 22:9). They felt that they had it in themselves to be holy like God and thus earn the benefits of their holiness.

The words of Genesis 6:5 appeared irrelevant to the Pharisees. Moses told how God saw that "every inclination of the thoughts of the human heart was only evil all the time." Moreover, the Pharisees easily deflected Isaiah's insight: "All of us have become like one who is unclean, and all our righteous acts are like filthy rags" (Isaiah 64:6).

5. How do these passages help us arrive at a proper application of Leviticus 11:45 above?

Lastly, we have seen how Paul the Pharisee was discredited by the Pharisees. No wonder! His God-inspired words declared that all have sinned and fall short of the glory of God, that nothing good lives in us, namely, in our sinful natures, and that in our sinful state we do not and cannot submit to God's law (Romans 3:23; 7:18; 8:7). Those words stand in direct contrast to the Pharisees' teaching about the law of God.

6. Read Galatians 3:1-11. Discuss how the Galatians were being influenced by Pharisaic type of thinking.

How, then, is the teaching of the Pharisees leaven? It begins by tapping into the essential flaw in our human nature. It convinces us that we can be like God and so merit his blessings. It sets us up for failure.

When we invariably fall short in any way, we think it must be because we simply need to try harder. It will lead us to rationalize away our own faults and magnify the faults of others. It will make us look for ways—extra things we can do—to cover our tracks.

This teaching, which determines our salvation based on what we do, can lead to a number of dead ends. Although it makes us want to do what God wants us to do, it drives us away from God because it in fact asks us to be our own god. It can lead us to a false sense of security—judging, contrary to God's perfect standards, that we are doing okay. Or, when we recognize how woefully we fail to meet those standards, it can and will drive us to depression and despair.

So the Pharisees' teaching, like leaven, permeates our very being. It leads us away from Jesus, just as it did with the Pharisees.

Points to Ponder

1. Although the Sadducees as a sect no longer exist today, their yeast has thoroughly permeated our world. Identify examples of modern-day Sadducean thinking.

2. Why might the yeast of the Pharisees be especially dangerous to us personally?

3. Look again at Luke 11:52. How did the Pharisees take away the key to knowledge? Compare with John 10:10; 11:25; 14:6

Lesson 9

"Woe to you, teachers of the law and Pharisees, you hypocrites!" (Matthew 23:13)

Setting the Stage

On a day recorded in Matthew 23, Jesus pronounced seven woes against the Pharisees. Read the words of introduction that Jesus spoke to the crowd (23:1-12). Identify three overriding attributes that seemed to influence the things the Pharisees said and did.

The Seven Woes of Matthew 23

The Pharisees began their charade by heaping up all kinds of extra laws that Moses never taught—a heavy burden on the common people—while they went about quite self-satisfied. With the showy religious trappings they wore, the seats of honor they coveted at banquets and in the synagogues, and the way they carried themselves in the marketplaces, the Pharisees liked nothing more than to appear important among the people. They wore titles such as "Rabbi" ("my master") as a show of their authority. In Jesus' words, they exalted themselves (v. 12).

- Think of examples of people today who exhibit a similar show of authority.

Jesus followed with the seven woes or judgments against the Pharisees. All of the woes except one specifically call them out as hypocrites.[17]

Woe #1 (v. 13)

By insisting that the people must earn their way into the kingdom of heaven, the Pharisees effectively locked the people out. Since the common people in general could not begin to practice the rituals with which the Pharisees fenced in the law, they were denied a place in the kingdom. Meanwhile, the Pharisees also locked themselves out. They got caught in the fence of their own making. They assumed they were better than the others and on their way to heaven. However, in counting their own merits as the way to the kingdom, they were fooling themselves and failing to see who they really were in their sins. Woe to such!

17 A *hypocrite* literally is a "play actor." The actors of the day wore masks as they pretended to be characters other than themselves. A hypocrite masks who he really is and pretends to be who he is not.

Woe #2 (v. 15)

We may not think of the Pharisees doing much mission outreach, but, in fact, they did seek to bring Gentiles into their religion. When they found some who would commit to their laws and practices ("proselytes," or converts from outside of Judaism who turned to Judaism and its practices), such persons often became fanatical in their adherence but were only driving themselves toward hell without the Savior. Many of the Pharisees themselves were not nearly as fanatic, but they were on the same road. Woe to them!

Woe #3 (vv. 16-22)

The hypocritical Pharisees were the blind leading the blind. None are so blind as those who refuse to see. So, in their self-inflicted blindness, Jesus also counted them as fools. He illustrated their foolish blindness by the way they treated swearing an oath. They would swear by the gold with which they decorated the sanctuary or by the gift they brought to the altar. They put more attention once again on what they did than on God who dwelled in the sanctuary, sat on the altar, and was alone to be glorified. Woe to those so misguided!

Woe #4 (vv. 23,24)

The Pharisees carried out the law's commands to the finest detail, as we have seen. As an example: God told Moses that "a tithe of everything from the land . . . belongs to the LORD" (Leviticus 27:30). The Pharisees, therefore, took a count of all the fine herbs and spices they used and gave one-tenth of them. As they became caught up in the forms and details of multiple specific legal rules, they began to lose sight of the matters that really counted, such as "justice, mercy and faithfulness." They strictly observed trifles (straining out gnats) while neglecting major matters (swallowing camels). Woe to those who pervert justice and mercy and faithfulness.

Woe #5 (vv. 25,26)

The Pharisees were all about ritual cleanliness. (And who of us would stand up against being clean?) So Jesus used their cleansing practices as an image to further illustrate their hypocrisy. They could scour the outside of a cup or dish ever so diligently, but that would accomplish virtually nothing if the inside was still unclean. So with the Pharisees: they carefully washed everything according to their customs, but inwardly they harbored "greed and self-indulgence." Woe to those who do not attend to the uncleanness within!

Woe #6 (vv. 27,28)

Hypocrisy: the bane of those who feel they must demonstrate their own worthiness! Having focused on the hypocrisy of the Pharisees, Jesus likened them to "whitewashed tombs." The outside of a tomb can look ever so clean and beautiful, but inside are the bones of the dead, and everything is unclean. To this day, the most well-groomed cemeteries still only cover death. So the Pharisees appeared righteous to the people, but "hypocrisy and wickedness" lingered inside of them. Woe to those who depend on outward appearances!

Woe #7 (vv. 29-36)

Speaking of tombs, the Pharisees made an effort to honor the prophets by decorating their graves and claiming that they would not have murdered the prophets as their ancestors did. Jesus, however, told them that they were no different than their ancestors. He would also send "prophets and sages and teachers" to them, and they would treat them the same way. And they did. Christians were scattered under persecution and disciples were martyred, in part at the hands of the Pharisees (not to mention their plot against Jesus the Messiah himself). Woe to those who spill the blood of the righteous.

The woes in Matthew's gospel sound unusually harsh coming from Jesus, but it was not the way Jesus wanted it. When the Pharisees revealed their hard-hearted, irreconcilable opposition to him, he spoke only the truth about their spiritual bankruptcy.

Speaking as the Son of God and Savior, he declared that he always wanted to gather them to him—"as a hen gathers her chicks under her wings"—but they were not willing (Matthew 23:37). The rift between the Pharisees and Jesus was created alone by the Pharisees.

Points to Ponder

1. What is the essential element behind all of the woes Jesus spoke in Matthew 23? Why is this such an important issue?

2. Who caused the rift between Jesus and the Pharisees? Read Matthew 23:37-39. What makes the rift irreconcilable?

3. Why does the law by itself inevitably produce hypocrisy? Read Titus 3:3-7; Luke 12:1,2; and Romans 7:21-25; 9:31,32.

Lesson 10

"Do you still not understand?" (Mark 8:21)

Setting the Stage

In Galatians 2:11-13, Paul called Cephas (Peter's Hebrew name) a hypocrite. Though the visitors from Jerusalem who threw everything into confusion weren't necessarily Pharisees, Peter and others, including Barnabas, consumed some of the leaven of the Pharisees. Describe what happened.

If Peter and Barnabas, pillars in the church, could end up on the wrong path, what about us?

I Thought I Saw a Pharisee!

The title for this chapter was originally the working title for this study. I was concerned with how we continue to use the term "Pharisee." Also, there is the claim of several that Pharisaic teaching ("leaven" according to Jesus) lies at the foundation of most religions today, including Christianity. Furthermore, how is it that you or I or anyone else should be spared the same criticisms levied against the Pharisees?

When we consider the leaven of the Pharisees, we need to look inward first before judging what we see outside of us. Can, or should, you or I be free from criticism for Pharisaism? Answer: We can't. I can't. All a person really has to do is look in the mirror. No, not the glass mirror in your bathroom! (Though, that may be bad enough.) I am talking about the mirror to the soul. Yes, the very thing that has been front and center in all we have observed, namely, God's law.

The law does not, as the Pharisees would have it, say to you, "Well done. You have never messed up, not even once, at least not bad enough to be concerned." Rather, every time you look it says, "See how you have messed up again and again and again." As the Pharisee Paul discovered, the law silences us from any boast we might want to make about our merit before God. "No one," he says, "will be declared righteous in God's sight by the works of the law; rather, through the law we become conscious of our sin" (Romans 3:19,20).

1. Our inherent sinfulness leads us to believe that people are basically good and we are able to earn God's favor by keeping the law. The theological term for that flaw is the *opinio legis,* "the opinion of the law." That inherent problem undergirds the teaching of the Pharisees. It is also the basic belief of all religions except Christianity. Unfortunately, it has spread (like leaven) throughout most of Christianity as well and adheres to our own sinful nature.

How do Romans 8:7; 1 Corinthians 2:14; and Ephesians 2:1 refute the *opinio legis*?

2. Defenders of Pharisaism consider the widely held *opinio legis* as evidence that the Pharisees have influenced all other religions and as verification that Pharisaism is true. How do you respond to that contention?

3. Many people would deny that our thoughts can be sinful. If we don't act on them in any way, they don't hurt others. How can they be sinful? How do the following passages refute that claim and demonstrate that we could never earn God's favor by keeping the law? See Matthew 5:21-27; Mark 7:21,22; and Romans 7:7.

Look at All the Hypocrites!

When a person thinks about what it means to see a *Pharisee,* it becomes obvious that there are Pharisees all around us. Jesus warned about the hypocrisy of the Pharisees. How many times have you heard someone complain of hypocrites in the church? It's true, isn't it?

When someone makes that complaint, however, the response might well be "Then you should fit right in." The very complaint reeks of hypocrisy. It judges others by outward appearances, without knowing all the facts surrounding their hypocrisy, and it judges persons' hearts, which only God can see. Still—I draw my own conclusions. I thought I saw a Pharisee, and he is I.

What's Wrong With Those People?

Jesus pointed out how the Pharisees looked down on those who didn't measure up to their standards, which they equated with God's standards. True, no one disputed that they appeared to be the most morally upright people among the Jews, probably among all people everywhere. Not only did the Pharisees look down on the common people, but they stacked up laws for the people that would guarantee that they would not be accepted among those bound for the kingdom of heaven.

Maybe our disdain for others is a bit more subtle than the example Jesus gave about the Pharisee and the tax collector, but more often than we like to admit (at least more than I like to admit), we validate our Christian living by comparing ourselves with others.

4. At a voters' meeting, after discussing the evangelism program, a man cautioned, "If we go all out on this, you never know what kind of people we might end up bringing into the church." Evaluate that statement.

5. Though we might never make the statement in Question 4, we probably think those kinds of things. Why, if we know such thoughts are wrong, do we still struggle with them?

Maybe the struggle is even more subtle: The call goes out at church for people to volunteer for a project. You are among the faithful ones who show up, but there are many others that seldom, if ever, come. How do you feel about them? Disappointed, angry, prideful by contrast? Maybe you go so far as to question the strength of their faith.

Naturally, we could make a case that some in any church have regrettable weaknesses that might make us wonder whether they really belong. They rarely, if ever, attend church and never serve. They display a bad attitude when encouraged to do better. Why even put up with them? Yes, I too have asked that question. I think like a Pharisee.

But then I hear God in his Word tell me to be kind, compassionate, merciful, forgiving, patient. Jesus tells me to be ready to forgive over and over again. The LORD says he will not break the bruised reed or snuff out the smoldering wick (prophesied by Isaiah (42:3) and fulfilled by Jesus in Matthew 12:20). Can we do less?

We are not denying that Jesus has commanded us to deal with manifestly sinful and unrepentant members. Yet that too requires humility and patient admonition (Matthew 18:15-18).

Look at Me!

The Pharisees loved to be recognized and honored. They taught humility but wanted people to see how humble they were. They expected to receive a high level of respect and be counted among the important people.

This is a tough one for us, isn't it? The more I think about being humble, the less humble I am. The moment I claim to be humble I am not. I gave a gift recently that no one saw me give. I wanted it that way. However, my sinful self still wished that someone would have seen me and wanted to praise me for it. I did—I saw a Pharisee.

There is a good reason for going through an exercise like this before looking back at the larger picture of religion and the Pharisees' influence on it. Only when we see that the problem of Pharisaism is an inherent problem with every one of us can we truly understand how it works like leaven wherever we look.

Points to Ponder

List ways that you see Pharisaic tendencies in your own life. Think of what you can do to avoid them.

Lesson 11

. . . not having a righteousness of my own that comes from the law, but that which is through faith in Christ—the righteousness that comes from God on the basis of faith. (Philippians 3:9)

Setting the Stage

If you have been a Christian for very long, it is likely that someone at some time has called you a hypocrite. It is much less likely that anyone has called you a Pharisee. Ironically, the more we study the Pharisees and their way of thinking, the clearer we may see that we have not remained free from their leaven.

The Larger Picture

In addressing the religions of the world, it is safe to say, for starters, that all religions other than Christianity go down virtually the same path as the Pharisees. They deny that Jesus is the very Son of God, the promised Messiah, the Savior of the world, and one with the Father and the Holy Spirit.

Though other religions may acknowledge a god, they teach that the way to his eternal favor must be earned. We must do his will to be saved. They cannot fathom the idea of another human being living and dying in our place to earn heaven for us, let alone a God who would give up his own Son to do that.

1. Some people believe that all roads lead to the same god. Read John 5:23; 14:6. How do those passages refute that statement?

To suggest, in turn, that the Pharisaic tradition is at the foundation of Christianity blatantly and arrogantly ignores the very issue that made the conflict between Jesus and the Pharisees irreconcilable. Wherever the truth of Jesus is taught as the Christ, the Son of God, and the only name under heaven that saves—people will be led to believe and be saved. The Pharisees denied and, to this day in the rabbinic tradition, continue to deny that truth.

However, it is equally true that the flaws of the Pharisees' teachings, the leaven to beware of, continue to threaten the basic foundation of Christianity. The Reformation in the early 1500s addressed some of the obvious issues: namely, the placing of tradition on a level with God's Word, the teaching that you have to do something for yourself to make up for your sins (e.g., the teaching about penance), and the denial that a person is justified freely by grace alone through faith in Christ without the works of the law.

Accordingly, in the spirit of the Reformation, many Christians to this day continue to take up the fight to keep the teachings of God's Word in their truth. We will guard, and should guard, the gospel of Christ with all our might and live a faith that reflects his truth.

2. Discuss ways that your congregation and you personally do or can do to take up the fight to keep the teachings of God's Word in truth.

But beware the leaven of the Pharisees. There is a bad joke that tells of a building in heaven that is completely walled in with no windows. When St. Peter is asked by some newcomers to heaven what it is for, he answers: "That is where the ____________ (*fill in the blank*) are, they think that they are the only ones up here." It should be said that no truly Christian tradition officially teaches such a thing. Some individual Christians, however, believe it and/or leave the impression that they do.

Whenever, in the name of Christ, a group of believers declares, "All you have to do is ____________ to be saved," it sounds like Pharisees talking. The gospel is about what God has done for us in Christ and by the Holy Spirit, not what we do for him. He brings his blessings to us through his Word.

Nevertheless, let's look at ways that Christians in all traditions, including our own, still run the risk of being Pharisees.

The Good Christian

What does it mean when someone says: "He is really a good Christian"? Before addressing that question, try responding to this statement: My Buddhist neighbor is more *Christian* than many Christians I know.

We all may think we understand what those statements mean in a proper way, but what do they say? They measure the validity, or at least the value, of a person's Christian faith by his works. The lesser or fewer the works, the more one's Christianity gets called into question. There is, in fact, a movement called Pietism that has plagued Christian churches over the years. It insists that a person must show a certain level of fruits of faith to be considered a true Christian. The Pharisees did just that.

3. How do the Scriptures, for example Romans 12:1, offer an entirely different perspective on good works?

Forgiveness

All Christians, it's safe to argue, believe the forgiveness of sins. Still, some will ask how many times must we forgive before our patience runs out? Even the apostle Peter thought there must be a limit until Jesus corrected him (Matthew 18:21,22).

Nevertheless, we hear a Christian say, "I'll never forgive them for that." Why? "Because they don't deserve it!" Or perhaps a person forgives but continues to hold a grudge or looks down on "less worthy" people with contempt. Or maybe they forgive others conditionally: I'll forgive you if you promise to do better.

4. How do we respond to such thoughts?

A Pharisee will expect a person to earn forgiveness, to make good choices deserving of forgiveness. Jesus teaches forgiveness for the unforgivable, given by grace through faith. Jesus sacrificed himself to guarantee that forgiveness.

Humility

You may have experienced the same phenomenon as I have: You are introduced to another Christian, perhaps someone checking out your church. In short order, your new friend begins to give you a litany of things he has done in the church. Although the speaker displays a humble demeanor, the words unmistakably sound like boasting. Yet at the same time, you would certainly welcome that kind of a Christian into your midst (more enthusiastically than another?).

5. The person just described could be a Pharisee. Explain how that could be so.

Theology

When questions of a church's teaching and practice arise, where do the questioners go for their answers? Naturally, it would seem, they would go to God's Word, to the Bible. Often, however, another element surfaces that seems to trump all else, namely, what the wise people of old taught or did. One person checks the church fathers. Another cites an expert from a theological school or a favorite pastor. Still another simply declares, "We always did things this way." Any one or all of these other elements can be helpful, but Scripture alone is the infallible basis for God's teachings. The Pharisees tended to let oral tradition and the opinions of experts outweigh the message of Scripture.

Worship

Nowhere, since God prescribed the ceremonial laws for the Jews of the Old Testament, does Scripture dictate how a believer must worship. With the coming of Christ, it is generally agreed that those ceremonial laws no longer apply. Nevertheless, ask a Christian how worship must or must not be done and you are likely to get some unexpectedly emphatic answers. Within a given denomination, some will advocate for one kind of worship in contrast to a different style of worship. They may allow that either can be acceptable while at the same time insisting that the one is definitely better than the other.

6. Discuss how to keep a discussion about worship style from sounding like a pharisaical debate.

Establishing the Fence

It may seem foolish that the Pharisees sought to build a fence around the law. As we have seen, they were meticulous in trying to prevent any erring. Some Christians seem to have a similar need to have specific sins defined in order to avoid them. Consider these kinds of questions: Is it a sin to say "golly," "gee," or "darn" or to use the expression "OMG"? Aren't they all just euphemisms for using God's name in vain? Is all dancing bad? If not, where must we draw the line between good and bad dancing? When giving offerings for the Lord (10 percent?), should they be set aside before or after taxes? What are legitimate reasons for divorce?[18] For example, when is a spouse guilty of desertion? Such detailed analysis of sin easily leads to legalism and a Pharisaic feeling of superiority for those who pay attention.

7. How far should we go to define sins? What's the problem in attempting to do that?

My Church Is Better

It is safe to say that every Christian denomination makes some case for having the teachings of Scripture right. By inference or direct challenge, others are wrong. And in fact, although the Pharisees actually taught that opposing ideas could both be right at times, logically some are right and some are wrong. Furthermore, it is important to guard the true teachings, as Scripture teaches.

The issue here is not about right and wrong and the importance of defending what is right. It is a matter of how we go about it. Do we humbly and diligently go back to Scripture while checking our own predispositions at the door? Do we use Scripture as a light to illuminate the truth or as a branding iron to bring the fires of hell against

18 The Bible teaches clearly that adultery and desertion are not God-pleasing and may lead to divorce. It does not, however, provide a detailed code of action.

anyone disagreeing? Do we boast of our orthodoxy or pray for wisdom and insight from God? Pharisees are more likely to boast.

My Church Is Flawed

People probably like their church more than they dislike it if they continue to stay in it. At times, however, it may not appear so. Some regularly complain to others about the flaws in the church. One thing we should know about flaws: if we look for them, we will find them.

8. Why might the white glove test in church lead to hypocrisy?

There is no perfect church. Even the Pharisees could not claim perfection but that they were working their way toward it. They were masters, however, at picking out the flaws in others.

Perhaps the biggest problem about finding flaws is that it leads us to ignore our own. We magnify the flaws we see about us and minimize or totally ignore our own. Remember Jesus' warning about seeing the speck of sawdust in another's eye while ignoring the plank in our own (see Matthew 7:3-5). That produces in us a certain Pharisaic, hypocritical disposition.

9. Obviously, we all want to improve, and the Bible encourages us to admonish one another. What is the difference between being judgmental versus being constructively critical?

Give Me a Sign

Have you ever wondered how many people (maybe you among them) secretly wish for a sign to prove God's gospel? The Pharisees ignored obvious signs (miracles) from Jesus and still asked him for a sign to demonstrate that he was who he claimed to be. People today are no different. We have God's Word, eyewitness accounts, the resurrection of Jesus and his appearance to many, the power of the Spirit at work through the gospel. Still we tend to think: I would be certain if only God would do something in my life personally to convince me.

Some spiritual leaders will capitalize on that desire for a sign. They will promise material and other blessings—if only a person's faith is strong enough, if only people will do God's will better. Then, they will see God at work.

But we don't need further proof than what we have, namely, that the Holy Spirit has worked faith in us through the Word to see and believe in Jesus as God's Son and our Savior. That holds good no matter what we encounter in this life on our way to eternity with Jesus.

Points to Ponder

1. List ways that you see Pharisaic tendencies at work in your own church. Think of how you and/or your congregation can counter them.

2. Discuss how the world's Christian religions have historically (and still today) succumbed to Pharisaic practices.

3. Discuss why virtually all who study the Pharisees from both favorable and unfavorable points of view conclude that the clash with Jesus was from the beginning irreconcilable.

Conclusion

You no doubt noticed that the writing in this study became much more personal as it moved from the historical and scriptural account of who the Pharisees were and what they taught to what their movement still means for us today.

I realize that I changed my tone, but I felt the need to do it because the issue of Pharisaism is, in the end, personal for us to this day. If this writing has accomplished nothing more, I pray that it helps us see that the problem of Pharisees, whose teachings lead people away from Jesus, is not just the irreconcilable differences that drove a group of people to oppose Jesus a couple thousand years ago. It is a problem inherent in each of us to this day because of the sin that has corrupted our natures. The solution to that problem is Jesus.

Gary Baumler

ADDENDA
Quotes, Factoids, and Stuff!

Pharisaic Oral Traditions

Cited by Edersheim in Volume 2:

> "It was ruled, that if anyone had performed the rite of hand-washing in the morning, 'with intention' that it should apply to the meals of the whole day, this was (with certain precautions) valid" (p. 13).
>
> Picking grain was considered a violation of the Sabbath. Plucking the ears was the sin of reaping. Rubbing them was sifting, grinding, or threshing.
>
> It was "forbidden to stop with a little wax the hole in a cask" (p. 56).
>
> Quoting Hillel: "[It is] sufficient ground for divorce if a woman had spoiled her husband's dinner" (p. 333).
>
> Citing well-known early Pharisee Akiba: It was sufficient [grounds for divorce] "if a man had found another woman more attractive than his wife" (p. 334).

Cited by Neusner:

> "The Pharisees held that even outside of the temple, in one's own home, the laws of ritual purity were to be followed in the only circumstance in which they might apply, namely, at the table. Therefore, one must eat secular food (ordinary, every-day meals) in a state of ritual purity as if one were a Temple priest" (p. 83).

Cited by Petuchowski:

> What God said to Moses on Sinai about the Torah: "There will come a time when the nations of the world will take the Written Law away from you, and claim that they (not you) are Israel. Therefore, I am giving you the Pentateuch in writing. But its true interpretation, the Mishnah, the Talmud, and the Haggadah, I am giving you orally. They will be what distinguishes Israel from the nations of the world." (p. 37). Mishnah, Talmud, and Haggadah are explained in the following sections.
>
> Hillel: "The ignorant man cannot be truly religious" (p. 179).

Cited by Bowker:

> Original Pharisee quote: "The rules about the Sabbath, festival offerings, and sacrilege . . . are as mountains hanging by a hair, for Scripture is slight, but the rules many" (p. 103).

Pharisees Origins

Quoted in *Pharisaism in the Making* by Louis Finkelstein:

> "A passage in Tosefts Yadaim, chap.2, . . . "shows conclusively that the Pharisees existed as a distinct group as early as the beginning of the fourth century B.C.E." (p. 175).
>
> At the time of the Maccabees, under the ruler Hyrcanus (135-105 B.C.), the Pharisees and the Sadducees were active rivals. The Pharisees were favored at first, but after a public breach with Hyrcanus, the Sadducees gained favor and power under Hyrcanus and his son, Alexander Jannaeus.
>
> Finally, when Salome Alexandra took power in 76 B.C., the Pharisees were again favored and gained significant influence politically and socially.
>
> By the time of Christ under Herod, however, the Pharisees no longer were major political players but held sway as the preeminent religious leaders among the Jews. Nevertheless, they still exercised a good measure of political influence.

One of the earliest sources of the Pharisees "clearly affirms the Pharisaic claim that their teachers alone were authorized interpreters of the Torah" (VIII).

The Pharisees often pointed back to the prophet Ezra as their inspiration. Ezra 7:10, "For Ezra had devoted himself to the study and observance of the Law of the LORD, and to teaching its decrees and laws in Israel."

Oral Torah in Print

The oral traditions were compiled in the Talmud in the second century C.E.

According to Herford, the Talmud comprises the Mishnah—the oral Torah written—and the Gemara—additional commentaries from Jerusalem and Babylon (pp. 70-87).

The types of teachings in the Talmud are:

1. Halachah: the preceptive portion that spells out the rules of conduct.
2. Haggadah: the nonpreceptive portion written for the purpose of edification. They were not written directly for the regulation of conduct but were considered lessons of truth and wisdom for God's children. They are said to be highly imaginative stories.

According to Edersheim in Volume 1, "The Halakkah indicated with the most minute and painful punctiliousness every legal ordinance as to outward observances, and it explained every bearing of the Law of Moses. But beyond this it left the inner man, the spring of actions, untouched. What he was to believe and what to feel, was chiefly a matter of the Haggadah" (p. 105).

Edersheim: "It is sadly characteristic that, practically, the main body of Jewish dogmatic and moral theology is really only Haggadah, and hence of no absolute authority" (p. 105).

The Promised Messiah

From Talmud Unmasked.com/chapter5.htm. Maimonides: "If all things he [Jesus] did had prospered, if he had rebuilt the

Sanctuary in its place, and had gathered together the dispersed tribes of Israel, then he would certainly be the Messiah."

Edersheim in Volume 1: "According to Jewish view the Messiah was to appear in outward pomp, and by display of power to establish the Kingdom" (p. 587).

Pharisaic Thinking

Herford: "The Jewish salvation assumed no sudden entrance of evil into the world, nor any sudden defeat of its power; no total depravity through the sin of Adam, no deliverance through a special agent conceived as both divine and human. It assumed the influence of God slowly working in all human lives, to bring about . . . the harmony which ought to be" (p. 168).

Abrahams: "God maintains his reverence by mercy, he as it were coaxes man to virtue by generously overlooking vice, and by making the sinner realize that he has not erred beyond the range of pardon" (p. 139).

Miscellaneous

The scribes and lawyers (or teachers of the law) in the New Testament were mostly, if not all, Pharisees.

According to the historian Josephus, six thousand Pharisees lived in the vicinity of Jerusalem in Christ's time. Besides the temple there were 480 synagogues.

"Pharisee" occurs almost 100 times in the New Testament:

Matthew	29	John	19	
Mark	12	Acts	9	
Luke	27	Philippians	1	(3:5)

Bibliography

Abrahams, I. *Studies in Pharisaism and the Gospels: Library of Biblical Studies.* Edited by Harry M. Orlinsky, Brooklyn, New York: KTAV Publishing House, 1967.

Boulton, Wayne G. *Is Legalism a Heresy? The Legacy of the Pharisees in Christian Ethics.* Mahwah, New Jersey: Paulist Press, 1982.

Bowker, John. *Jesus and the Pharisees.* Cambridge University Press, 1973.

Charlesworth, James H. and Loren L. Johns, editors. *Hillel and Jesus: Comparative Studies of Two Major Religious Leaders.* Minneapolis: Fortress Press, 1997.

Davies, W. D. *Introduction to Pharisaism* of Facet Books Biblical series, Philadelphia: Fortress Press, 1967. (Preface by John Reumann, Luther Theological Seminary.)

Edersheim, Alfred. *The Life and Times of Jesus the Messiah,* Vols. I and II, Grand Rapids: Wm. B. Eerdmans Publishing Company, 1956.

Ezell, Douglas and S. Taylor. "Pharisees." http://mbsoft.com/believe/txc/pharisee.htm (accessed 06/30/04).

Finkel, Asher. *The Pharisees and the Teacher of Nazareth.* Leiden, Netherlands: E. J. Brill, 1964.

Finkelstein, Louis. *Pharisaism in the Making: Selected Essays.* Brooklyn, New York: KTAV Publishing House, 1972.

———. *The Pharisees: The Sociological Background of Their Faith.* Vol. I, Philadelphia: The Jewish Publication Society of America, 1962.

Herford, R. Travers. *The Pharisees.* Boston: Beacon Press, 1962.

Huie, Bryan T. "Who Were the Pharisees and the Sadducees?" http://users.aristotle.net/~bhuie/pharsadd.htm (accessed 6/30/04).

Kern, Kathleen. *We Are the Pharisees.* Scottdale, Pennsylvania: Herald Press, 1995.

Koelpin, Wyn. "The Pharisees – An Old Religious Fraternity." 1980, archived in the Wisconsin Lutheran Seminary Essay File.

Neusner, Jacob. *From Politics to Piety: The Emergence of Pharisaic Judaism.* 2nd ed. Brooklyn, New York: KTAV Publishing House, 1979.

Petuchowski, Jacob J. *Heirs of the Pharisees.* New York: Basic Books, 1970.

Osborne, Larry. *Accidental Pharisees.* Grand Rapids: Zondervan, 2012.

Toppe, Carlton. "A Time Honored Warning against Present Dangers to the Church from Pharisaism." 1948, archived in the Wisconsin Lutheran Seminary Essay File.

The Lutheran Confessions

Bible dictionaries

Wikipedia

Internet searches

The Bible